CATS

GALLERY BOOKS
An Imprint of W. H. Smith Publishers Inc.
112 Madison Avenue
New York City 10016

This edition first published in U.S.
in 1990 by Gallery Books,
an imprint of W.H. Smith Publishers, Inc.
112 Madison Avenue, New York, New York 10016

ISBN 0-8317-9576-X

Printed and bound in Spain

For rights information about the photographs in
this book please contact:

The Image Bank
111 Fifth Avenue, New York, NY 10003

Producer: Solomon M. Skolnick
Author: Lee Server
Design Concept: Lesley Ehlers
Designer: Ann-Louise Lipman
Editor: Sara Colacurto
Production: Valerie Zars
Photo Researcher: Edward Douglas
Assistant Photo Researcher: Robert V. Hale
Editorial Assistant: Carol Raguso

Title page: **A mother cat feeds with her two kittens. The maternal instinct is quite strong in cats, and mother cats have been known to care for the young of other species.** *Opposite:* **The cat's reputation for curiosity is well-deserved and can lead it into all sorts of mischief.**

The special friendship that exists between cat and man is now over 4,000 years old – and going strong.

No animal in history has had a comparable hold on both our hearts and our imagination. The cat is at once the familiar domestic object of our affection and amusement, and the great unknowable, a mysterious stranger in our midst. It has been the diminutive member of the family in countless millions of households, as well as intriguing inspiration for centuries of artists, thinkers, and theologians. Since the time it deigned to leave the wilds some four millenia ago, the cat has been the star of our poems and paintings, stories and songs, myths, magic, and religion.

The cat's appeal to mankind is a phenomenon of extraordinary dimension and color. While it has been domesticated, adopted, adored, and rhapsodized, the cat has, as well, been worshipped as a deity and feared as a devil.

Top to bottom: Cats enjoy each other's company in relaxation as well as play. This Virginia barn cat is a first-rate mousecatcher. Cats have worked on farms for centuries. An open window can prove dangerous for a cat, especially if a bird happens by, but with their flexible skeletons and balance control, cats can survive falls from extreme heights. *Opposite:* A cat on its own can grow bored and listless. Cats are usually much happier and active with a companion.

The cat's hearing and vision are acute. They are able to see and hear far more than humans. *Opposite:* Cats have endless ways of amusing us—sometimes just by doing nothing at all.

The Abyssinian is a regal, intelligent cat. It is friendly and affectionate –
a perfect family cat – but quite active, needing a home with lots of space.
Opposite: Because of the shape of its ears, body, and tail, the Abyssinian
is thought to be a direct descendent of the sacred cats of Ancient Egypt.

The American Shorthair can come in almost any color combination. Shorthair kittens can be quite enormous. *Left:* The cameo tabby American Shorthair is one of the most familiar looking of American cats. They are quiet and gentle, though strong and active creatures.

Why has the cat been able to capture so much of our attention? Some of the reasons are readily apparent: it is a creature of beauty, grace, and intelligence.

The cat has been called nature's most beautiful invention. While this may be arguable, few would disagree that the sight of a warm-eyed, shiny-coated cat is an aesthetically pleasing experience. Its grace is likewise

The British Blue is the most popular and award-winning of the British Shorthair breeds. It is the oldest natural breed in Great Britain. *Right:* Crossbreeding of the traditionally blue British Shorthair has produced varieties in over eighteen colors and patterns.

undeniable. Anyone who has observed the sinuous rhythms of a cat in motion – its effortless efficiency and strength in leaping onto a surface several times its height – knows that the cat's movements are as elegant as any in the animal kingdom.

As for intelligence, while we may be guilty of anthropomorphizing our cats to a fanciful degree (that is, ascribing human behavior and thinking to our pets), the cat has the large and convoluted brain typical of intelligent mammals.

Most cat owners can attest to just how smart a cat can be. Cats will open door latches, get milk from a closed bottle, start an electric can opener to signal mealtime, turn the tap in a sink to get water, and approach all sorts of new problems, finding ways to solve them.

And the cat's emotional life is equally sophisticated. Certainly man's fascination with the feline has something to do with the way it seems to express humanlike feelings and moods: anger, affection, melancholy, anxiety, jealousy. . .love. And with the cat's rich vocabulary of sounds and tones, who can blame us for thinking it is genuinely trying to communicate with us?

Top to bottom: **Most typical of the Burmese cat, the Sable is rich brown in color. Other colors of Burmese have developed through selective breeding, although some consider these breeds to be Malayans. The Blue and the chocolate brown Champagne are classic examples.**

The Ocicat is a paradox: it has the look of a wildcat—its name is derived from the ocelot—but a sweet and gentle temperament makes it an ideal housepet.

Cats have become adept social creatures, learning to get along with other animals, be protective and gentle with small children, and otherwise adapt to their circumstances in a very civilized manner. And yet the cat is also a natural predator – a hunter.

Whether a cat is the scruffiest denizen of the alley or the most pampered show cat, it has inherited a predisposition toward hunting, trapping, and killing prey. More than one genteel cat lover has had to face this distressing fact when their pampered pussycat has strutted home with the mangled remains of a mouse or bird dangling from its mouth. Even more distressing is that domestic cats, who do not hunt for survival, usually toy with their prey before killing it. It is part of the great paradox of the cat: it is domesticated and yet retains a touch of the wild.

And perhaps therein is the root of our eternal fascination and speculation about this mysterious creature.

The Exotic Shorthair is a cross between the American Shorthair and the longhaired Persian. It has the beauty and personality of the Persian without the grooming problems. *Left:* **This bronze Mau is of Egyptian derivation – the word is, in fact, Egyptian for "cat." It is a muscular cat, designed for hunting.**

The brown tabby and mackeral tabby are Exotic Shorthairs. These animals are docile, low-key, and very good with children.

This Exotic Shorthair shows the round, glowing eyes characteristic of the breed. Eyes are set well apart, as are the ears with their rounded tips.

The Manx comes from the Isle of Man off the coast of England. Normally lacking a tail, it has been the source of much colorful speculation. Legend has it that the Manx was the last creature to come aboard Noah's Ark and its tail was snapped off by the closing door.

The History of the Cat

The history of the cat goes back twelve million years. Soon after the Ice Age, when our own primitive ancestors were established, most of the members of the three genera of cat, *Panthera*, *Acinonyx*, and *Felis*, were distributed throughout the world.

The first category, *Panthera*, includes the six big cats: the lion, tiger, panther, jaguar, snow leopard, and clouded leopard. *Acinonyx* is the category for the cheetah, the fastest of all animals. Under the third category, *Felis*, are the great majority of cats – thirty in all – including the bobcat, ocelot, lynx, various other wildcats, and *Felis catus* or *Felis domestica*, the domestic cat. While few wildcats are ever truly domesticated, most domestic cats have the capacity to turn feral.

As best as scientists can determine, the direct ancestor of our modern domestic cat is *Felis libyca*, the African Wildcat, native to North Africa and much of Asia. Other wildcats probably

Top to bottom: **The recently bred white Oriental Shorthair is a cross between the Siamese and the white Domestic Shorthair. The "man-made" Oriental Shorthair, almost identical to the Siamese, comes in a vast range of colors – over 400 different shades. Oriental Shorthairs are intelligent, graceful, and affectionate.** *Opposite:* **The white, odd-eyed Devon Rex has been officially recognized in America only since 1979. Distinctive characteristics include its wedge-shaped face, pixieish expressions, and suede-like coat.**

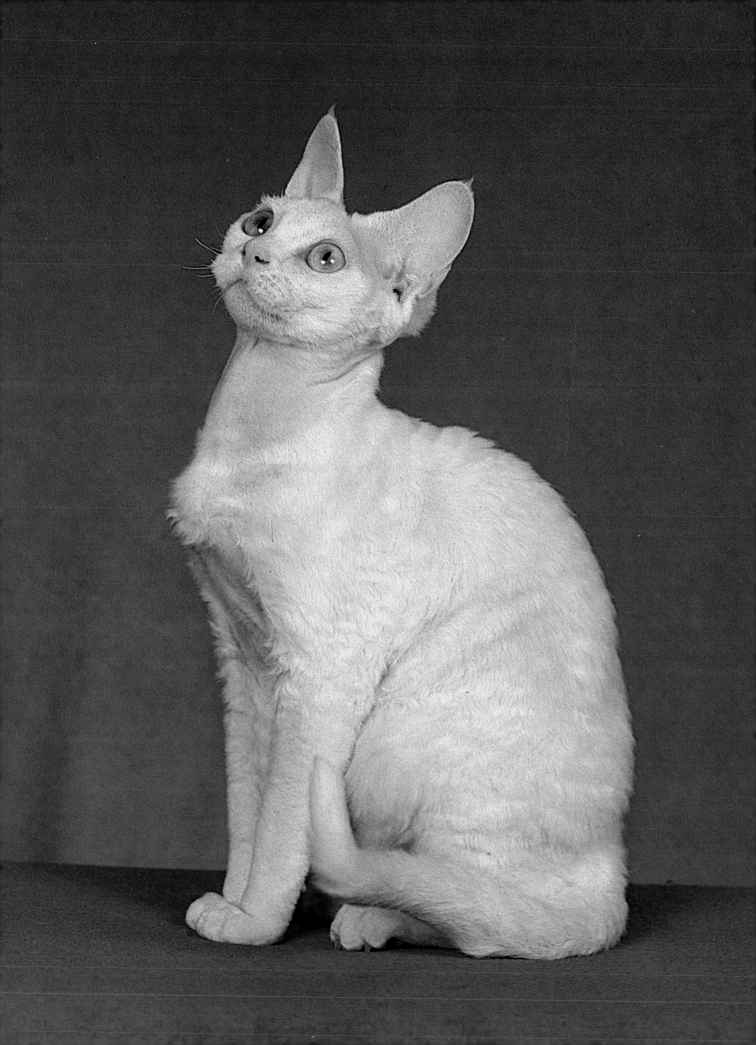

Preceding page: The Russian Blue has a heavy, shimmering blue coat, tinged with silver. It is one of the quietest, most introspective of cats, warm to its owner, but distant to strangers. *This page:* The Scottish Fold gets its name from its ears, which are droopily folded over. The breed is derived from a pair of kittens born in Scotland in the 1960's.

The round, soulful eyes of the Scottish Fold give it a sweet and sympathetic expression. In fact, it is one of the gentlest, sweetest-tempered of all cats. *Opposite:* A gathering of eight-week-old Scottish Fold kittens. Ears are straight at birth, but begin to fold when the kittens are about one month old.

contributed to the domestic's ancestry: the *Felis chaus* or Jungle Cat, also native to North Africa and Asia, and *Felis manul*, also known as Pallas' Cat, found in the rockier regions of Asia.

The birthplace of the domestic cat is Ancient Egypt. The first clear evidence of domestication dates back to 2000 B.C., when inscriptions and pictures referred to the Egyptians' growing relationship with the cat. The African Wildcat was a lissome, light brown, striped animal, very similar to the domestic tabby. It is likely that these and other wildcats were kept as exotic pets for a time before the development of the domestic cat.

A typical Siamese cat has a cream-colored body with darker-colored "points" on the head, tail, and legs. With the Siamese Blue-Point, the body is white-blue with dark blue points. *Opposite:* Siamese cats have a strong, distinct personality. Although some consider them to be arrogant, they are loyal and intelligent companions.

While it would be interesting to give the domestic cat's birth a bit of the magic or intrigue we have long associated with them, the reality is decidedly more prosaic and practical. In the 18th Dynasty of the New Kingdom of Egypt, the silo was invented, allowing for the storage of vast quantities of grain. Where grain was stored, mice and rats were soon to be found, followed in due course by cats. In Ancient Egypt, cats were excellent vermin catchers (as they remain today), and saved the Egyptians' crops. Because they were too valuable to return to the wilderness, they were placed in captivity, and the process of domestication began.

The Singapura is a native of the Southeast Asian island of Singapore where it is considered a mere "street cat." A rare breed in America and Europe, it is shy, but full of curiosity. *This page:* White feet give the Snowshoe its name. Developed in America, this cat was crossbred from bicolored American Shorthairs and Siamese. *Below:* The coloring of Snowshoe kittens may take several weeks to develop. They are playful—even for kittens—and grow to be highly sociable and devoted to people.

Hard as it is to believe, the cat's somewhat dirty job of killing mice and rats led to its enshrinement and deification. It was a sacred animal, the star of various religious ceremonies. Revered by all, cats were mummified at death and buried in special cat cemeteries. Mummified mice were buried beside them to provide tasty sustenance on the long journey to the hereafter. Cat killers were put to death, and when a cat passed on, its human family showed their grief by shaving their eyebrows.

Many of our English cat words and nicknames derive from the African genesis of the domestic. The Arabic word *quttah* is the likely derivation for the Roman "*catus*," as well as the modern "cat." The word "puss" or "pussy" has come to us from the Egyptians' cat-headed goddess variously known as Push, Bash, and Bastet. Our "tabby" was originally another word of Middle Eastern origin, *utabi*.

Preceding page: This household tabby strikes an outdoor pose, reminding us that his distant cousins are the tiger and the leopard. *This page, top to bottom:* When cats are already acquainted, a typical greeting is nose rubbing, accompanied by some body rubbing and sniffing. In a confrontation, there is usually one aggressor and one defendant, with typical body posturing according to their roles.

Although cats will fight for any number of reasons, they generally get along well together and are capable of forming complex and supportive social relationships with their own kind. *Opposite:* Cats enjoy climbing from a very young age. Although climbing is often part of the hunt for prey, they will also climb for the sheer fun of it.

During the era of the cat's veneration, it was forbidden to export them from Egypt, but crafty foreigners, seamen, and merchants with their own grain supplies to protect, smuggled cats to Greece, India, and elsewhere. As Egyptian religious beliefs slipped away from animal deification and took on the gods of the Greeks and Romans, cats were openly traded. The notion of the cat as a sacred object, however remained in other parts of the world. Goddesses were depicted as cats in numerous cultures from Britain to Africa to China.

The cat's holy heritage had its down side, however, when spiritual beliefs and superstitions changed and the cat evolved into a symbol of evil. From the dawn of Christianity and throughout the Middle Ages, cats were feared as incarnations of the devil and cohorts of witches and black magicians. Many thousands of cats were put to horrible deaths in this long and dreadful era.

Preceding page: Cats have excellent balance and coordination. A part of the inner ear called the vestibular apparatus helps give them a precise sense of position in space. *This page:* A kitten may have no trouble climbing up a tree, but getting down is another story. Its claws are not designed for the descent and fear or indecision may leave it immobilized. There is often no alternative to the owner getting a ladder and rescuing the stranded pet. *Below:* Because their back legs are quite powerful, cats can easily jump five times their own height.

Preceding page: This yellow tabby appears ready to explore a neighboring yard. Nearly all cats are territorial, but toms, or male cats, have a wider, less concentrated range. *This page:* Cats are predators by instinct and often strategically observe birds, insects, and other small creatures. The best way to keep a cat from killing birds is to tie a small bell to its collar, thus alerting prey.

The unusual American Curl (a black and a brown tabby) has oddly-shaped
ears. Gene mutations continue to produce new and unique breeds of cat.

There was a short-lived respite from this persecution in Europe when cats saved much of the continent from a plague caused by Asian rats, but fear and hatred took hold again. Happily, in the Far East and Muslim Asia, the cat remained a creature of veneration and a prized pet. By the seventeenth century, Europe had at last come back to its senses and the cat returned to favor. Books such as *Les Chats* and *Puss in Boots* helped bring on a new, more secular cult of the cat.

Throughout the eighteenth and nineteenth centuries, the cat began to figure more prominently in European and Western art and literature. Its status was confirmed by Queen Victoria of England, owner of three blue Persians. Cat shows and competitions began in the 1870s and breeders began experimenting, developing an array of more colorful and exotic breeds of cat, a trend that continues to this day. In this century, the popularity of the cat in the Western world has grown tremendously and shows no sign of slowing down.

This page: **Another recent breed, the Cymric (the Welsh word for Wales) is a long-haired variation on the tail-less Manx. Despite its exotic Oriental name, the Balinese is a native of the United States, developed by American breeders.**
Opposite: **Another "designer cat," the flame point Himalayan was bred from strains of long-haired cats and Siamese. Breeders were seeking a cat with the point pattern of a Siamese and the lush, heavy coat of a Persian. The flame point is one of the newest colors for the breed.**

Preceding page: This seal point Himalayan has the standard brown "points" of the Siamese. The breeding of pedigree Himalayans began in the U.S. in the 1950's. *This page:* The Kashmir is a solidly colored variation on the Himalayan. These "self chocolate" cats are an offshot of breeders' development of chocolate-point Himalayans.

The Maine Coon is a native American, and one of the oldest breeds known in North America. *Left:* Popular for centuries on New England farms, Coons are large, robust, easygoing family pets, but unrelenting mousers. Because of their hearty nature and wild look, the origin of the Coon has been the subject of many folk tales. One legend has it that the original Coon was a cross between a wild cat and a raccoon. *Opposite:* The red classic tabby Maine Coon.

A pair of brown tabby and white Norwegian Forest Cats. The breed has achieved championship status in recent years, but its history goes back to Norse mythology. *Opposite:* Like the Maine Coon, the Norwegian Forest Cat has a heavy coat to protect it from cold northern winters.

The Nature of the Cat

As with so many other aspects of its existence, the cat's biology and its behavior patterns have been surrounded by legend and whimsical speculation – some true, some false, some slightly exaggerated.

We say that a cat "has nine lives." The reference to the number nine probably comes from that number's significance in ancient rites and religions. The expression itself refers to the cat's agility and speed in escaping harm and its legendary ability to survive falls from great heights, landing on all fours and calmly – at least from the outside – walking away.

A cat's ability to right itself in a fall and land on all fours involves a series of almost simultaneous reflexive movements. Its muscles, skeleton, and senses all work together with lightning speed, coordinating a response. As it is falling, a cat will instantly level its head, then twist the front half of its body till it faces the ground, rotating its back half and using its tail as an adjustable balance. Back arched to help absorb the shock, the cat hits the ground with a perfect four-pawed landing.

Top to bottom: **Three versions of the beautiful, luxuriant Persian: a red and white bicolor, a red classic tabby, and a tortoiseshell. Persians come in a rainbow of colors and patterns, which are categorized in six divisions of color for the purposes of competition. *Opposite:* For many, the Persian is the epitome of the pedigree cat. It has been a feature – and winner – of many cat shows and competitions.**

Preceding page: A silver Persian shows off the plush, cuddly body and large, warm eyes that make this breed so beloved by cat fanciers. *This page:* This trio of silver Persians is just eight weeks old. Kittens have a short coat when born, but begin to develop their rich, long hair after about six weeks. *Below:* This black and white bicolor Persian has the copper eyes of all particolors and bicolors of the breed.

There are records of cats falling from heights of 100-feet and more and surviving. But cats, alas, are not immortal, and they are more often seriously or mortally wounded in such falls.

The eyes of the cat are another area of colorful speculation. Cats cannot actually see in the dark, but they do have excellent three-dimensional vision, and their night vision is at least six times more acute than that of humans. A cat's eyes have special characteristics – because of its nature as a hunter, the nerves are extremely sensitive to movement.

The gentle eyes of this blue Persian kitten indicate the breed's sweet, affectionate personality. It is a quiet, docile pet, but demands attention—its long coat should be groomed daily. *Opposite:* Blue Persians are often considered the "perfect" example of the breed. They were popularized as the pet of royalty by England's Queen Victoria, who owned three.

A cat's pupils are similar to the lens in a camera. In bright light, they become small, cutting out the glare. In the dark, the pupils enlarge to make the most of available light. The cat's eyes come equipped with a special membrane called a haw which acts as a supplementary eyelid, lubricating the eyes during illness.

The idea that a cat's eyes glow in the dark is, of course, no myth. This illumination occurs when light hits upon a mirror-like tissue in the eyes called the tapetum lucidum.

It was long believed that cats were completely color blind. Recent scientific experiments have shown that this is not true, but that the distinguishing of colors seems to be of little interest or value to the cat. Vision, however, is the cat's most important sense. Kittens are blind for the first week or ten days of their existence and take several months to learn how to properly use their sophisticated ocular equipment.

The Ragdoll is a complex hybrid, the result of matings between the seal point Birman and the white Persian, and a further mating between this offspring and the Sable Burmese. It has existed since the 1960's. *Below:* The Ragdoll gets its name from the way it seems to relax and go as limp as a ragdoll when held. It is docile and very people-oriented, and loves to play. *Opposite:* The Somali is really a longhaired Abyssinian. These cats were first seen in Abyssinian litters, the result of a recessive gene re-emerging. They are now specifically bred and are the softest–voiced of all cats.

Preceding page: The cat is by nature a hunter and is never happier than when prowling the outdoors for prey. *This page:* The hunting instinct can be triggered by almost any small moving object.

The folktale that cats can predict earthquakes and other natural disasters has a good deal of truth behind it, due to another of the cat's keen senses – hearing. Cats have extremely delicate and sensitive ears, and are able to hear much more distant and higher pitched sounds than humans. So, they do indeed have an early warning system when it comes to earthquakes and other similar conditions. Cats, no doubt, prefer using their delicate ears for less stressful situations – many cats have been known to enjoy soothing music and will listen to it raptly for long periods at a time.

The Breeds of Cat

The vast majority – more than 90% – of all cats are not pedigreed or purebred. A pedigree cat is one that has been mated only with its own breed, or a hybrid that is bred with other cats under specific genetic guidelines.

There is certainly nothing wrong or inferior about non-pedigree cats. All cats are individualists, and each individual

A farm cat oversees his domain. Farm cats have been working quite effectively as vermin catchers for centuries. *Below:* The cat has a well-deserved reputation for balance and coordination. But these skills are only partially inherent – they must be perfected through trial and error. *Opposite:* The cat's teeth can be quite deadly when necessary. Mice and other small prey are often dispatched with a single lethal bite.

These pages: Cat's eyes are perhaps their most complex feature. Legend has it that they can see in the dark and, perhaps, this is only slightly an exaggeration. The extreme sensitivity of the cat's retina makes its vision at least six times more acute than human vision.

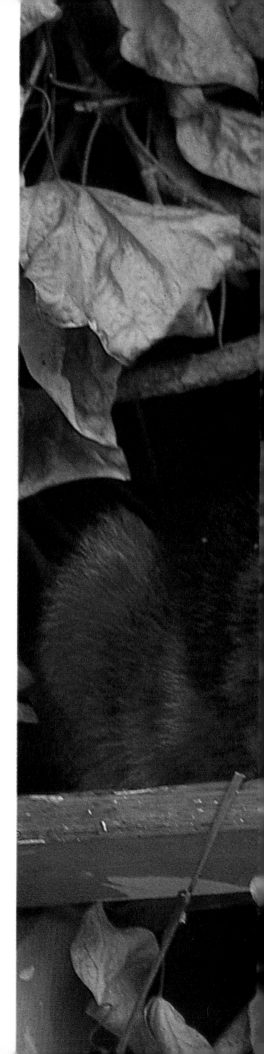

cat has his or her own personality and special qualities. In fact, any number of cat lovers, given the choice, would stick with their scruffy, adopted stray or their down-to-earth housecat of ambiguous ancestry over the most ribbon-winning of purebred show cat.

A breed is defined by such factors as geographic birthplace, body type, color, and hair. Some breeds are natural evolvements. Others are man-made, by crossing two (and sometimes more) breeds to form a new one – the so-called "designer cat." Some breeds have distinctions much greater than color pattern or hair length, such as the tailless Manx cat, the Scottish Fold with its peculiarly folded-over ears, and the wrinkled, hairless Sphynx.

Purebreds come in three basic body types or builds: the Svelte or Oriental, the Intermediate, and the Cobby. The first group includes all of the slim, fine-boned breeds such as the Siamese, the Singapura, and the Oriental Shorthair. In the Intermediate group are a wide variety of mid-size cats, from the Maine Coon to the Egyptian Mau to the Abyssinian. Finally, the Cobbys are the large or plump-looking breeds such as the Persian, the Himalayan, and the Exotic Shorthair.

Top to bottom: **A young cat gracefully maneuvers through a wicker chair. Cats are sinuous and able to negotiate all sorts of narrow and awkward openings. This is due to their flexible skeletons, particularly the highly mobile backbone.**

The expression on this brown tabby's face indicates that it has been alarmed. Cat's ears are very sensitive, especially to highly-pitched sounds, and can be easily damaged.

The colors of all breeds fall into one of five divisions: solids, particolors, tabbys, shaded tipped colors, and point restricted.

Because purebreds are so carefully monitored by specialists and breeders, it has been possible to isolate all sorts of characteristics according to breed, from personality quirks to potential health problems and special care needs. A person shopping for a pedigree cat can study this research to find the cat that perfectly matches his or her personality.

Cat breeding is really only a century old and the art and science of breeding is developing all the time. In the future we can look forward to even more colorful and unusual versions of this fascinating creature – the cat.

A cat's whiskers – also known as vibrissae – serve several functions. As feelers, they help the cat to judge its surroundings and changes in the atmosphere. They can also express a cat's mood, depending on their position. *Left:* A cat will hiss when another cat invades its territory as both a warning and a threat.

The position of a cat's ears is one more way it communicates. Ears that are pulled down flat signal an angry cat; straight up signals alertness.

Index of Photography

DEP. LEG. B-22.456-90